Let's Fly

FIGHTER JETS

by Wendy Hinote Lanier

I0887603

FOCUS READERS

www.focusreaders.com

Copyright © 2019 by Focus Readers, Lake Elmo, MN 55042. All rights reserved. No part of this book may be reproduced or utilized in any form or by any means without written permission from the publisher.

Focus Readers is distributed by North Star Editions:
sales@northstareditions.com | 888-417-0195

Produced for Focus Readers by Red Line Editorial.

Photographs ©: guvendemir/iStockphoto, cover, 1; trubach/Shutterstock Images, 4–5; VanderWolf Images/Shutterstock Images, 7, 16, 29; Everett Historical/Shutterstock Images, 8–9, 10; Dawid Lech/Shutterstock Images, 13; Paulo M. F. Pires/Shutterstock Images, 14–15; Viktoriya Popova/Shutterstock Images, 19; Nadezda Murmakova/Shutterstock Images, 20–21; Paul Drabot/Shutterstock Images, 23; Peter R Foster IDMA/Shutterstock Images, 25; Graham Bloomfield/Shutterstock Images, 26–27

Library of Congress Cataloging-in-Publication Data
Library of Congress Cataloging-in-Publication Data
Names: Lanier, Wendy Hinote, author.
Title: Fighter jets / by Wendy Hinote Lanier.
Description: Lake Elmo, MN : Focus Readers, [2019] | Series: Let's fly | Audience: Grades 4-6. | Includes bibliographical references and index. | Identifiers: LCCN 2018030374 (print) | LCCN 2018030882 (ebook) | ISBN 9781641855112 (PDF) | ISBN 9781641854535 (ebook) | ISBN 9781641853378 (hardcover) | ISBN 9781641853958 (pbk.)
Subjects: LCSH: Fighter planes--Juvenile literature.
Classification: LCC UG1242.F5 (ebook) | LCC UG1242.F5 L385 2019 (print) | DDC 623.74/644--dc23
LC record available at https://lccn.loc.gov/2018030374

Printed in the United States of America
Mankato, MN
October, 2018

About the Author

Wendy Hinote Lanier is a native Texan and former elementary teacher who writes and speaks for children and adults on a variety of topics. She is the author of more than 30 books for children and young adults.

TABLE OF CONTENTS

U.S. NAVY
U.S. NAVY
U.S. NAVY
U.S. NAVY

CHAPTER 1

AT THE AIR SHOW

It is a busy day at the Miramar Air Show. Hundreds of airplanes are on display. The sky is filled with airplanes, too. Fighter jets perform stunts high in the air. They flip and roll as the crowd cheers.

The Blue Angels soar across the sky at the Miramar Air Show.

The Miramar Air Show is the largest military air show in the United States. It is held in San Diego, California. The event lasts three days. More than 700,000 people attend each year.

Many school groups come to the show. Students watch planes fly.

FUN FACT

The Blue Angels are the US Navy's flying stunt team. The planes fly as a group. They form patterns in the air.

These F-4 Phantom jets belong to the Greek Air Force.

They tour the displays. Students even meet pilots. They learn about flying jets for the military.

CHAPTER 2

JET GENERATIONS

Jet engines were invented in the 1930s. They made airplanes go much faster. People began making fighter jets soon after. Germany flew the first fighter jet in 1942.

The German Messerschmitt 262 was the first successful fighter jet.

The F-80 was used by the United States during the Korean War (1950–1953).

By 1945, other countries had fighters as well. They included the Soviet Union and the United States. These airplanes were the first **generation** of fighter jets.

Second-generation fighters first appeared in the 1950s. The new jets used **afterburners**. They could fly faster than the speed of sound. They also carried **radar**.

FLYING FASTER THAN SOUND

Some planes reach supersonic speeds. That means they fly faster than the speed of sound. Sound travels approximately 768 miles per hour (1,236 km/h). When planes fly faster than this speed, they create a loud noise. The noise is called a sonic boom.

Radar shows where other planes are. It also maps the ground below. The new jets could also drop bombs. And they used guided missiles. The missiles could find targets on their own.

Third-generation fighters were built in the 1960s. Thanks to new

FUN FACT

The Nighthawk was built in the 1980s. It was the first stealth fighter. That means it was hard to see with radar.

The MiG-29 is a fourth-generation fighter built by the Soviet Union.

building methods, the jets could change direction faster.

Fourth-generation fighters began in the 1970s. Their engines were more powerful. Flight controls improved, too. For the first time, the controls used computers.

CHAPTER 3

BUILT FOR SPEED

Fighter jets are built for speed. A jet's wings slant back toward its tail. This shape reduces **drag**. Less drag means the jet can fly faster. And it can make sharp turns.

The sleek design of Portugal's F-16 helps the airplane speed through the air.

PARTS OF A FIGHTER JET

Jets get power from engines. A powerful fan pulls air into the front of the engine. The air is mixed with fuel and burned. Hot gas shoots out a nozzle at the back of the engine.

Many jets use afterburners. An afterburner goes near the back of the engine. It adds more fuel before the gas reaches the nozzle. This step produces even more power. The jet can fly faster.

PILOT TRAINING

Some of the best fighter pilots are part of Top Gun, the US Navy's pilot training program. The program began in 1969. It teaches pilots about flying and fighting in jets. A movie was made about the program in 1986. The movie was a huge hit.

Most fighters seat one person. The pilot sits in the cockpit. Pilots use **instruments** to steer. Some jets have a second seat behind the pilot. The person in this seat helps with many tasks, including weapons.

Fighter jets carry many kinds of weapons. Missiles and guns are

FUN FACT

Fighter pilots must be between 34 and 40 inches (86 and 102 cm) tall when sitting down.

A fighter jet's cockpit is filled with many different instruments.

often hidden inside the plane's body. That way, they create less drag. And it is harder for radar to spot the plane.

NAV1 110.95 ↔ 112.60
NAV2 109.50 110.95
FOB 32GL
ETA __:__UTC
GS 0KT
FPL - ACTIVE FLIGHT PLAN
TRACK UP
POWER % 0
RPM 0
FFLOW GPH 0.0
OIL BAR 0.0
OIL TEMP°C 20
COOLANT °C 20
GEARBOX °C 20
VOLTS 23.6
ALTR AMPS 0
BATT AMPS -12
21 FUEL °C 21
FUEL QTY GAL
12 26 14
T110
T108
LKSA
LKKT
P861
LKLN
LKST
20
LKPL PLZEN
P31
LKRY
PISEK
L726
Z650
LKHV
LKPM
PSK
5
LKBU
CZECH REPUBLIC
LKKL
LKPR
LKBE
LKTC
L984
Y444
LKVL
LKKB
80NM
ENGINE
MAP
NEW WPT
VIEW
VNV PROF
CNCL VNV

CHAPTER 4

FIGHTER JETS TODAY

Today, pilots fly fifth-generation fighters. These jets are almost invisible to radar. Their cockpits use many computer screens. The screens surround the pilot. Some screens show where the jet is.

Computer screens give airplane pilots many kinds of information.

Some screens show where the jet needs to go. Other screens help the pilot find and aim at targets. Screens also track the jet's **altitude**.

In 2014, some fighters gained a new safety feature. It is an automatic crash avoiding system. The system keeps track of the jet's

FUN FACT

The F-22 Raptor is one of the top fighters in the world. It can fly more than 1,300 miles per hour (2,092 km/h).

Much of the technology the United States uses to build the F-22 Raptor is top secret.

position. If the jet is about to hit the ground, the system takes over.

It steers the jet. It keeps the jet level until the pilot is in control.

People continue to design better fighters. In the future, fighters may work with **drones**. A pilot would lead a group of drones. The drones

MANY MODELS

The F-35 Lightning II is a US plane. This plane comes in three **models**. Each can do different tasks. The F-35A takes off and lands the usual way. But the F-35B can perform short takeoffs. It can also land vertically. The F-35C is designed for aircraft carriers.

An F-35A fighter has a wingspan of 35 feet (11 m).

could gather information. Or they could destroy a target.

HOW IT WORKS

HIDING FROM RADAR

Fighters often use radar to look for enemy planes. Radar works by sending out radio waves. When the waves bounce back, radar collects them and uses them to form a picture. The picture shows if planes are near.

However, an object that scatters or takes in radio waves will not show on radar. For this reason, aircraft designers choose shapes that scatter radio waves. They make jets with jagged edges and curved surfaces. They may also cover jets in a thick paint. The paint takes in radio waves. As a result, the jets do not show up on the radar image.

An F-117 fighter's shape makes it hard for radar to detect.

FOCUS ON
FIGHTER JETS

Write your answers on a separate piece of paper.

1. Write a paragraph explaining how a jet engine works.
2. Would you want to be a fighter jet pilot? Why or why not?
3. Which generation of fighter jets began using computers for flight controls?
   - **A.** second generation
   - **B.** fourth generation
   - **C.** fifth generation
4. What would happen if fighter jets were easy to spot with radar?
   - **A.** More jets would crash into the ground.
   - **B.** More jets could be found and shot down by enemies.
   - **C.** More jets would fly with drones.

5. What does **perform** mean in this book?

*Fighter jets **perform** stunts high in the air. They flip and roll as the crowd cheers.*

A. change color
B. watch a show
C. do an action

6. What does **reduces** mean in this book?

*This shape **reduces** drag. Less drag means the jet can fly faster.*

A. makes something smaller
B. makes something bigger
C. makes something stay the same size

Answer key on page 32.

GLOSSARY

afterburners
Parts that add fuel to a jet's exhaust to increase the jet's power.

altitude
Height above the ground.

drag
The force of air pushing back against a moving object.

drones
Aircraft or ships that are controlled remotely or operate on their own.

generation
A stage in the development of a device, machine, or vehicle.

instruments
Devices used for collecting information, navigating, or controlling the movement of an aircraft.

jet engines
Engines that produce power by burning a mixture of fuel and air and sending out a stream of hot gases.

models
Different versions of a vehicle.

radar
An instrument that locates things by bouncing radio waves off them.

TO LEARN MORE

BOOKS

Omoth, Tyler. *Fighter Pilots in Action*. Mankato, MN: The Child's World, 2017.

Scheff, Matt. *Jets*. Minneapolis: Abdo Publishing, 2015.

Sutherland, Mark I., and Amy C. Sutherland. *Being a Blue Angel: Every Kid's Guide to the Blue Angels*. 2nd ed. St. Louis: Dunrobin Publishing, 2017.

NOTE TO EDUCATORS

Visit **www.focusreaders.com** to find lesson plans, activities, links, and other resources related to this title.

INDEX

Answer Key: 1. Answers will vary; **2.** Answers will vary; **3.** B; **4.** B; **5.** C; **6.** A